Thoughts on Creation

Curtis B Cline

Thoughts On Publishing

520 S Crestway Wichita, KS 67218

thoughtsonpublishing@gmail.com

Printed in the United States of America by IngramSpark, Inc.

ISBN: 978-0-997525922

Foreword

Thanks to anyone who picks this book up and even casually looks through it. Because by doing so, your view of creation and your place in it will forever be changed. Expanding your mind, broadening your view and evolving as a child of creation is the point of this book.

This is not a work of fact supported by assumptions. This is a study of possibilities supported by facts as understood at this time.

I am not asking you to believe anything presented here. I am asking that you consider the possibilities and come to your own conclusions. Above all as a child of creation, I just encourage you to be yourself and have fun.

Namaste'

Curtis Cline

Dedication

As my legacy to the world, I leave behind four sons, all good men of whom I am very proud and love beyond measure.

To my sons, and the rest of humanity, I leave these thoughts. I believe that books and ideas have a way of going where they are needed. I hope that these thoughts take on a life of their own, move about as needed and make the world a better place.

TABLE OF CONTENTS

IN THE BEGINNING

My first subject is in the beginning   where it all began, how it began, and why did it all start? When discussing creation, I think there are a couple of things that must be observed in order to discuss creation effectively:

Put aside the concept of time and space, outside of our everyday world, time and space really don't have any purpose except to confuse and clutter things up. Just for the time being, put time and space somewhere else.

The next thing we avoid is using the name God. When a person uses the name God it brings in religion and all the biases that we carry from childhood. This does not allow us to see clearly.

It has been said it is possible that creation has always been here and will always be here.   I think acceptance

1

of this fact is exremely important for a person who is trying to understand creation or at least our part of it.

Consider this, if we were ants with about a two month lifespan and we saw human beings with an 80 year lifespan, what would we think? An ant would say that humans have always, do and will always exist. My conclusion is this, for the purpose of this discussion. I acknowledge that I lack the mental faculties to fully comprehend the infinite. It is a given, for the purpose of this discussion, that creation has always existed, does exist, will always exist.

I see creation as a force. I don't know what it is, but it is powerful and very much exists. I would say that nothing exists outside of creation. This is a hard concept to get one's mind around if one looks at it from the outside. I can, however, envision creation from the inside. I see light totally filling every space as I look around extending into infinity. Everything is filled with light, light is energy, and energy is creation. Consider this, there can be nothing outside of creation. Everything that exists, has ever existed, or will exist must exist within creation.

I suggest that we exist outside the concept of time. We are all timeless. We are all immortal because energy cannot be made or destroyed; it can only be changed. As people, we experience a change of state when we die. Our physical body decomposes and, given time, will return to its various elements. We can be cremated, hacked up, put through a blender, whatever you want. The smallest you can get is back down to subatomic particles or if you want to go with a molecule, which is the smallest unit that still retains its identity, that s all good. As I said, when we finish our lifetime, at whatever point that is, however that occurs our body   gets recycled back into the system, on this physical plane of existence.

At physical death our unique unit of energy, which I like to refer to as our Divine Essence, moves on to non-physical planes of existence in creation. Each of us is a Divine Essence, a specific, unique, unit of energy in creation. Consider an analogy of drops of water in an ocean; we are each a drop. Each drop is unique and has its own existence but is still part of the ocean. It is home in the ocean, accepted, a loved part of the whole. Each drop is totally aware of everything around it.

It is my thought that when we die our physical body gets recycled and our Divine Essence returns to creation. We are unique little specks of energy that move to a different plane of existence, where we are once again, aware of being part of the whole. Physical death is nothing to be worried about. We are not being destroyed; we are only going through a change of state from our Divine Essence inhabiting a physical body for a brief period, to our natural state as part of creation. Once again, we only get a change of state. This understanding, for me, takes the fear out of the death experience.

It has been said that there is no heaven and hell; there's just going home. In addition, someone else said that we all make our own heaven or hell. Both statements are true. More on that in the discussion of Heaven and Hell.

A question comes to mind that bears discussion, which would be. Why would creation with all its perfectness and all its completeness, create? The simple answer is that it must! Otherwise, what would be the point of creation s existence? It is creation s nature to create, to build, to transform, to change, to destroy, to tear down, and start over again. That is why creation has to create, because it has to do what it does.

BLACK HOLES

Another thought on the universe is this: scientists study black holes and how they work. We know anything that goes into a black hole is not coming back out, including planets and galaxies. I submit to you that one day scientists will discover that black holes are the recyclers of the universe. It seems that everything in nature is circular. All things of a physical nature, on the physical plane, experience birth, life, death and return to its origin to begin the cycle again. This is true from plants and animals to galaxies and universes.

In at least one major belief system, it is discussed that the universe was created by the great cosmic elephant . As it wandered through creation, it pooped, and the universe emerged from the dung of the cosmic elephant. I used to think this was quite an amusing story. In my ignorance, I didn t recognize the symbolism being used to describe an indescribable event in terms that people of the day could relate to. With greater understanding, now I am amazed that what we today would consider the primitive mind of several thousand years ago, without technology, would have an intuitive understanding of the origins of our universe.

Now the story makes sense to me. What is the biggest thing they knew of? Elephants! To primitive man they were unstoppable, unbelievably powerful and all they do, all the time, is wander around and continuously eat. When the material the elephant has eaten completes its trip through the digestive system of the elephant, yep, big poop!!

When things, including stars and galaxies, are drawn into a black hole, scientists tell us that everything gets compressed together into a chunk of material containing everything from an entire universe. This is where our technology ends; scientists don't know what happens after that.

It is my thought that when the ball contains enough material, the black hole can't hold it any longer, so it falls out on the other side. Kaboom, the black hole births another universe, as described in the Big Bang theory of how our universe was formed. Yes, the chunk of matter contains everything needed to make a new universe. All the minerals, elements, gases and all other things it takes to create an entire universe. Everything is still there and totally recycled. This system is constantly in operation in creation.

LAYERS OF CREATION

The Asian community had it right when they talked about the analogy of the thousand petal Lotus. As it blooms, we find one petal inside another petal inside another. The analogy is useful as a physical manifestation that helps us get our finite minds around an infinite subject. My thought is that creation goes on infinitely and that life of many kinds must certainly exist within many layers of creation.

This begs the question…. What is meant by "layers of creation"? An analogy would be to consider creation as an infinite number of radio frequencies, each being a level of existence (for example, the physical plane that we live within is one level of existence). Now imagine that radio frequencies that are higher or faster exist beyond our level into infinity. The same thing happens below our frequency as, lower or slower, frequencies exist below us to infinity.

Some people speculate about the existence of life as we know it elsewhere in our universe, and undoubtedly someday we'll find out. However, if we ask a similar question about whether life exists as we know it on another layer of creation, the answer must certainly be yes. With infinite layers of existence in creation, this would make possible infinite manifestations of existence.

Long before we become mature Creators of our own cosmos, we will have developed the ability to place our "awareness" at will, anyplace we want. Imagine the possibilities for space or even time travel. If we could send our awareness to another location, on our plane of existence or perhaps other planes of existence. We will travel to any location desired, with the speed of thought, and enjoy full or even enhanced perception of what is going on at that location. We will be unnoticed by inhabitants at other levels of existence with a different vibratory   rate than our own because their perception is not tuned to our vibratory rate. Another consideration; we will be unable to interact because of our differences in vibratory rate. And this difference in vibratory rate will protect us from being infected or bringing back any of their diseases, which we would almost certainly not be ready to deal with.

What do you think?

LOVE VIBRATION

The "Love Vibration" is not the highest frequency in the spectrum of infinity. However; it is the highest vibration in our creation. How do we know this? Because the love vibration is the source of all lower frequency vibrations below it. This means that everything in creation is brought into being by the love vibration slowing to the rate needed to express a certain something.

For example, consider that it is the love vibration that slows to create the sub-atomic particles, that make the molecules to express basic elements of nature, i.e. oxygen, nitrogen etc.. Creation uses these basic building blocks to create our physical bodies and to provide for us through the system that we call Nature. Things creation provides for us would be water, trees, animals everything in nature that we use to eat, build homes and live our lives. All things in creation are manifested using the love vibration. Consider that our sun is an expression of the love vibration and the light energy from the sun that plants use for photosynthesis is sustained by the love vibration. In nature it is accepted that the DNA provides the blueprint of how things grow and heal. It is the love vibration that makes up the DNA and provides the basic elements to function.

Scientists have determined that everything in creation is vibrating all the time and the difference in vibratory rates is what differentiates things. The love vibration is the force that powers, sustains and controls all of creation.

We communicate with Creator via the love vibration. Our thoughts while generated by us on the physical plane are of a non-physical nature. This means that our thoughts, powered by emotion, reach out to the Creator to request the things we want in our lives. Creator created the love vibration and sustains it, therefore; **Creator is love.**

FREE WILL

The importance of free will is often overlooked when considering the creative process, in fact without free will there can be no creative process. Because to be creative we must have the ability to choose between options to create new outcomes.

This also explains why we can only learn, experience and evolve when on the physical plane where the "veil" is put between our mind and Creators' mind. While free will is a gift beyond measure, it is not without consequences. The consequences being that we have to deal with the outcomes of our creating, whether we like them or not.

Notice that after making decisions and creating an outcome in our lives, now we have an entirely new set of circumstances to deal with which forces us to make more choices, more creating. This is a never ending process throughout our lives on the physical plane.

Consider also that the gift of free will is a tangible expression of Creators' love for us and expectations for us to learn, experience and mature as creators. Free will is the final ingredient we need to create. We are empowered by Creator to create, which is why we have the ability via abstract thought, to use our imagination and visualization faculties to express our desires.

We are empowered to create by being given full access to the "Love Vibration" which is the highest vibration in creation which can manifest anything we can imagine. However; we are not aware of our connection to the Love Vibration. A person must do the work to develop an awareness of self, others and the world. Then spend time in meditation to willfully connect with the Love Vibration to be a conscious creator.

WILL

The use of "willpower" to accomplish our goals is very different from the "free will" we use to choose between options. Will is used in concert with the ability to concentrate. Both of these powerful tools for creating are learned by spending time in the silence. You can see how the daily act of entering the silence requires us to exercise our will to do the work. Throughout the session we use both will and concentration to stay focused.

The positive effects of having a strong will in everyday life can't be overstated. During times of distress when we are being tested by life it is our will that we use to answer the challenge. When we are working out it is will that keeps us going when we are feeling tired and want to stop. It's will that we use to get us out of bed for that early morning run and will that we use to get our homework or that monthly report for work done on time.

So, you probably get the point by now, for success as a creator manifesting the things you want in your life, spend time in the silence and challenge yourself in other ways, to develop your will. You will be glad you did.

EMOTION

Like free will and will, emotion is an often overlooked yet integral part of the creative process. Think of the word emotion as, E = energy in motion. The ability to capture the power of our emotion when trying to create makes a huge difference in our success as creators.

Consider that the untrained mind or "Monkey Mind" is a slave to emotion. Any emotion is allowed to drive the mind into a frenzy! However; to the creator who has spent time in the silence and has control over their mind, emotion can be a powerful tool.

Let's take time to explore our relationship between the physical and the non-physical in our daily lives. One example is, our mind (non- physical) controls our brain (physical) which generates electrical impulses (physical) which end up as thoughts (non-physical). Another example, we sense something using either our five physical senses (physical) or via the energy body which surrounds us (non-physical). Whatever it is we sense, induces an emotional feeling (non-physical) which directs our brain to respond (physical) affecting breathing, heartbeat, all sorts of chemical reactions etc. You can easily see how we interact with the non- physical all the time.

I submit to you, that in learning how to create effectively, we learn to use the brain to produce thoughts which induce an emotional response. This is how we access the non-physical in a powerful way via our emotions. A successful creator will give subconscious a clear, well defined thought. Then power the subconscious into creation using their emotional energy. This is why a passionate, near desperate plea for assistance is much more powerful than a request made without emotional energy.

Here are some final thoughts on emotion for your consideration. I think we only experience two emotions; love and fear. All emotional feelings that we experience are degrees of these two emotions. For example, the love we feel for our children is very strong. Feelings for friends may be less intense. And the clerk we find pleasant at the store is another feeling. (Note; all these are positive love feelings).

An example of negative or fear emotions include; extreme anger, jealousy or hate when we fear that someone may take something or someone away from us. Or we may feel frustrated or shame, fear that someone will discover we don't know how to do something, making us ignorant or vulnerable. Shame being fear that someone will find out we have done something that will cause them to lose respect for us or show that we lack integrity.

MY RELATIONSHIP WITH CREATION

There are infinite levels of existence, as many levels of existence as there are vibratory rates to infinity. For example, if you have one cycle per second, two cycles per second, three cycles per second to infinity, there is a level of existence at each cycle and many levels of awareness in each level of existence.

We are put at this particular level of existence because when we arrive at the physical level (birth) we rapidly "forget" our connection with creation. It's as though all the distractions of being born, learning to work our physical body, and countless other distractors puts a wall between us and creation. We quickly lose awareness of our connection with creation; however, this is an illusion. It is a physical impossibility that we could ever be disconnected from creation. Because we are children of creation, I am a manifestation of creation because I am physically made up of the stuff of creation.

Consider that just because we are on a physical plane of existence and that most of the time we are not thinking about creation, this does not disconnect me from creation. It is creation that keeps everything vibrating. It is creation that keeps us breathing, hearts beating, and digestion working, and so on. It is creation that provides for all our needs, all the time. Creation wants us to be happy, grow, learn, evolve, and become creators ourselves.

For us to be separated from our Creator, we would have to be outside creation. Stated simply, creation has always existed, does exist, and will always exist. It is such a simple truth, yet somehow hard for us to grasp that creation is all that there is. One more time.......

CREATION IS EVERYTHING THAT IS!

There are those in positions of authority in our world who say that we are manifestations of creation. Then in the next breath they tell us that we must act and do according to their instructions, or we will be separated from creation for eternity. If these authority figures actually understood what they say, they would recognize that they are contradicting themselves. It is exactly their first statement, that we are all manifestations of creation, made from the stuff of creation, which keeps us from ever being disconnected from creation. Any statement or idea contrary to that is false. Anyone who would say such a thing needs to get their money back from whoever taught them about creation because they really don't understand what they're saying.

It should be obvious to the most casual observer why we must temporarily lose awareness of our place in creation when on the physical plane. Unlike when we exist in non- physical form, where we have direct awareness of creation which enables us to understand everything. When we are on the physical plane and lose our aware connection to the whole of creation, it empowers us to experience, learn and create here, in the physical that is not found in non-physical levels of existence.

Here we don't already know the answer to everything because of our direct awareness with creation. On this level of existence, when we ask a question we have to figure it out. This forces us to develop and use our creative power and free will to manifest the things we want. It also allows us the freedom and the responsibility to learn how to create our lives on this plane of existence. We will develop all the tools it takes to be powerful creators. Our challenge and goal on the physical plane is to re-establish our intimate relationship to creation here and to take control of our existence on this physical plane. Our thoughts are our tools for this work.

Our thoughts are energy. The power of the clear, well-defined, thought sent out into creation with emotional drive is limitless. Emotions are what propel our thoughts out into creation. The emotion of being desperate and needing assistance, for example, has much more power going out to creation than saying, without emotion, "Gee, I sure wish someone would come save me." The E in emotion is the energy that gives power to our creating. More energy means faster, more powerful manifesting of our requests on this physical plane of existence.

Basically, creation is just looking for more opportunities to create. When this creation nature is used in concert with our subconscious mind, amazing things happen.

As our subconscious mind responds to our commands, it does not judge or question. Subconscious mind is totally trusting of our conscious mind. If we state that we want or need something, no matter how foolish, subconscious mind does not judge. It assumes we know what we want and why we are asking for it. All of us, especially new manifesters need to choose wisely. This means using the tools of free will, discipline and awareness that we have developed through meditation. By exercising our abilities to focus and discipline ourselves, we learn to become aware of our thoughts and what we're creating. When we have become adept at that, then we can focus our thoughts and send out a, well-defined, thought with powerful emotion behind it, into the universe. The subconscious constantly works in the universe, making our desires known, and creation tries to fulfill our request. Sometimes we like what we get, and sometimes we do not. We get what we ask for and then we complain.

Who is at fault here?

WHY ARE WE HERE?

We are here to learn, experience and develop the tools needed to be creators. Only on the physical plane can we experience, learn, and evolve. When we are on non-physical levels of existence, we are in direct connection to creation and know the answers to everything already.

At this plane of existence, the physical plane, we are still connected with creation because we are a manifestation of it. But there is a veil, if you will, which forms between our mind and creation as we become distracted by learning to operate our body, speak, learn culture, and find our way here. It is by developing the mind and becoming adept at using our brain that we are able to penetrate the veil, experience our connection to creation and see clearly again.

Consider that our origin, as a unique speck of creation, was in the mind of the Creator. At the will of Creator, we were thought into existence, "birthed" in the mind of Creator. We remained in the mind of Creator until it became our turn to leave our safe, happy home and go make something of ourselves.

This was our first introduction to the physical plane of existence, what a shock! Always before in our existence we were in harmony with creator via the "love vibration." Because of this connection, we knew and understood everything; nothing was beyond our grasp. Coming to the physical level of existence changed all that. Although we maintain our connection with creation because we are manifestations of creation, our vibratory rate is too slow for us to keep up with the love vibration. We were no longer able to know and understand as before.

On the physical plane, we feel things like pain, both mental and physical. We experience confusion, frustration and are overwhelmed. We just don't understand why things are and what we are supposed to do with stuff, all very frightening to us. We are motivated to change things just to survive here.

One of our most frightening experiences here on the physical plane is the feeling of isolation. Luckily for us, although we are unaware of it, creation is still watching out for us. The love vibration continues to keep our hearts beating and our bodily systems functioning, while creation continues to supply all our needs. Of course, we are unaware of all of this because of our slow vibratory rate.

Creator knew that we would need assistance if we were going to make it. He gave each of us a subconscious mind to help us and act as liaison between us and creation. At that time we were unaware of the subconscious mind, but it didn't matter. Whenever we thought about what we wanted or needed, subconscious headed out into creation to bring it about. Subconscious is non- physical, so it can speak to creation via the love vibration, to make things manifest for us. It wasn't long before some became aware that when they thought about things, especially if they planned and had a well-defined image of what they wanted, things happened.

This was the beginning steps of us becoming conscious creators. At the time we didn't realize we had the gift of thinking in abstract. This is what enables us to be creative and think about things that we have neither seen nor experienced before. We were unaware that we had become aware of our ability to create or "manifest" things in our lives.

Creator, in his infinite wisdom wants us to learn to create. We have been creating and manifesting things in our lives every day and as we use our creative ability, we change our vibratory rate.

We have a feel for good and bad, experience compassion and plan for the future. All of these learning experiences help us develop our mind and other creative tools like free will, discipline, and awareness. We experience suffering and want throughout our lives. This is no accident, and it isn't Creator being mean to us for his pleasure. No, suffering and the desire to satisfy our needs is what motivates us to practice and become more adept at creating or manifesting what we want in our lives. Sounds pretty good so far, doesn't it? Well, here comes the difficult part.

With knowledge comes responsibility. As we mature as creators, we have opportunity to make some good and some not so good choices. We do this by using: "Free Will" (This is the "with knowledge comes responsibility part"). We are allowed, by Creator, to make any decision we want; however, we must deal with the outcome of our decision. If we chose to do bad or negative things, then we get those outcomes. If we chose to do good or positive things, then we get to experience those outcomes as well. The choice is all up to us.

Not only are we held accountable in the short term, which would be dealing with ramifications of our actions here on the physical plane. We are also held accountable long term for our decisions on the physical plane.

We discussed that everything is made up of vibrations. Well, that includes thoughts of all kinds that we have every day. Now we must discuss our faithful, non-judgmental, companion and servant, subconscious. In addition to duties of attending to us, acting as liaison with Creator and going about manifesting things for us. Subconscious also records everything in our entire life that we experience on the physical plane.

Throughout our lifetime on the physical plane, we have our own unique vibration. Our vibration is affected by many things such as the food we eat, how we take care of ourselves, and our thoughts (The thought part is what picks up the good or bad vibrations associated with the choices we make). All of these vibratory inputs affect our unique vibratory rate all the time. Now for the long term we mentioned earlier. When our existence on the physical plane is finished we experience physical death. At that instant our subconscious, which has been recording every positive and negative vibration for our entire life, determines our final, unique vibratory rate. This final unique vibratory rate is neither good nor bad; it just is. What is important is that this vibratory rate determines where our Divine Essence will be, until given another chance to enter the physical plane to learn, experience, and evolve.

The connection between levels of creation and our unique vibratory signature at our physical death is this: When we die, our physical body returns to nature and is recycled; however, our Divine Essence, which is non-physical, heads out into creation at the speed of thought, straight to the level of creation that matches our unique vibratory rate. (More about this on the chapter titled Heaven and Hell). The point is that some levels of creation are pretty sweet and some are not so sweet depending on the vibratory rate. In either case, we had free will, we got to choose, so we did it to ourselves. There we stay until we return to a physical plane to continue experiencing and learning, to continue the process.

Consider the possibility that we continue the process of experiencing, learning, and raising our unique vibratory rate until our vibratory rate matches the vibratory rate of our origin, in the mind of Creator. However, now instead of taking our seat inside the mind of creator, we are recognized as a peer, a fully functional creator.

More on this is in the chapter Man as Creator, but the point I want to make now is that the answer to "Why are We Here?"

We are just trying to get HOME!!

Final thoughts on raising our vibratory rate...a great man is quoted as saying;

"There is no need for temples, no need for complicated philosophies. My brain and my heart are temples, my philosophy is kindness."

The Dali Lama

If there was one thing we could practice during our time on the physical plane to improve our vibratory signature, it would be to be kind.

If kind is too much for you, start out by being nice. Gradually work your way towards being considerate, then being kind will come to you. Remember; being kind means not only to others, and all things, but to yourself as well.

MEDITATION

The art of meditation can be whatever you make it. Meditation is either the simplest easiest thing you've ever done. Or it can be one of the most complex, difficult undertakings a human being could ever try.

There are many types of meditation. The trick is to find the one that resonates with how you like to do business. Some types of meditation use a mantra. This would be a phrase or a word or a name repeated until one enters a trance-like state to listen actively.

Some types of meditation involve looking intently at a spot on the wall or a pencil point or some other fixed object. Some techniques encourage you to focus on the breath at a point just below your nose. And others just encourage you to sit quietly and observe your thoughts with detachment while listening actively.

Regardless what technique you use, eventually you will go into meditation, and I call this "entering the silence". You will calm your mind and begin to listen intently for whatever creation sends to you. It is this time spent in the silence that empowers us to access the love vibration and communicate with creation.

Entering into the silence is for your mind what going to the gym is for your body. It's in the silence that we do the hard work of developing the mental muscle required to become creators. It is in the silence that you will learn discipline and will and develop the ability to visualize clearly. It is only by developing this mental muscle that we are able to send a well- defined thought, out into creation powerfully.

Just like at the gym for your physical body, you will get out of it in proportion to what you put into it. The positive effects of daily time in the silence cannot be overstated. I would submit to you that every time a person enters the silence to do work, their vibrational rate increases just a little bit.

It's possible the daily practice of meditation and consistently being kind to oneself and to others, makes a significant difference in one's vibratory rate over a lifetime. This has a significant impact on where our Divine Essence relocates to when we exit the physical plane of existence. My personal meditation technique is added at the end of the book.

AWARENESS

At first look this may seem like a strange subject to write a section about. Of course, we are aware. We work, drive, take care of business etc. we are aware. I submit to you that many, maybe most, people are going through their lives paralyzed from the neck up. In these people the "Monkey Mind" is in control, which means they are out of control. Their thoughts follow one another through association one to the next, not through conscious choice or selection. This is the awareness we are discussing here. Cultivating awareness is one goal of daily meditation practice.

- People who are aware know how they feel about things on an emotional level, are sensitive to energies in those around them and feel compassion for others deeply.

- Aware people notice their self-talk, whether it is positive or negative, will chose to remain positive and use discipline to make it happen.

- The aware person will control their eating habits to maintain a healthy body and mind.

- Aware people notice pollution of all kinds in their environment. And try to reduce or avoid it.

- The aware person notices and limits negativity in their lives from personal biases, conversations with others and from sources like television and music.

- An aware person senses others' energy. This can include emotional state, thoughts or motivation.

- People sense the higher vibration of an aware person and respond to them differently.

- Aware people see beauty in creation.

- Aware people feel con-
  nected to all living things.

These attributes are part of being an aware person. There are more, as you will discover. Spend time in the silence.

Enjoy!

RELIGION

What good is religion? Well, you might think I am cynical about religion and I am; however, religion has its part to play. It is a shame some religious groups don't stress development of the mind as part of their program. Many Eastern beliefs practice daily meditation and provide guidance and instruction to people about how to think. Notice, I said "how" to think, not "what" to think. Here in the West, most religions dropped the ball on teaching meditation or assisting people to learn to think. All they do is give out a full bag of guilt – you are born in Original Sin, yet they don't ever teach you how to rise above that, how to reconnect with creation and how to be happy. The function of religion, in my opinion, in addition to teaching folks to think, is to establish parameters within society whereby those who chose to live within these parameters can live relatively sanction free. For those who chose to live outside the parameters, the law of the land provides sanctions for their behavior. More on Law in the next section. Although Creator inspired man to establish social parameters, man has tailored the rules to work to the advantage of the few in power. I see a lot of man's influence in the mix, and anything man creates has a lot of potential for disaster.

Some organizations say that we must have a member of their staff talk to Creator for us. Once again in my ignorance, I thought this amusing and a strategy to exploit the unaware. But with greater understanding I submit to you that a "new" creator may feel unworthy or inadequate to talk directly to Creator.

By going through the mechanics of telling a staff member their needs and desires a clear thought is formed in the mind of the new creator. Then the new creators' subconscious takes this well-defined thought and heads out into creation to fill the request. Possibly this clear well defined thought would not have been accomplished without the process of communicating it to the staff member. In addition, the staff member's next task is to add their emotional plea, to satisfy the needs of the new creator.

Enter another confusing part for the new creator. The staff member just finished acting as intermediary between the new creator and Creator. Then the staff member directs the new creator to go and daily spend time in the silence contemplating things. I think this is similar to directing a person to go meditate daily, except without the how-to's. The thinking new creator might ask "if you just talked to Creator for me, why am I being told to go spend time in the silence?"

While confusing for the new creator, I think this is a transitional point in new creator's development. I submit to you that after enough time in the silence, the new creator will feel their own connection to creation.

It is my thought that when the new creator develops skill and awareness of connection with Creator, they will no longer feel the need to use a staff member to satisfy their needs. This period of change causes confusion for the new creator for a while, but it passes. The reason for the confusion is the change in relationship between new creator and staff member. This change many times is accompanied by the ending of the relationship.

Like any other relationship in our lives, when it's over we can expect to experience the following grieving process:

- Denial
- Bargaining
- Anger
- Depression
- Acceptance

This grieving process occurs time and again in our lives, to a greater or lesser extent, whenever we experience change. All part of learning and experiencing on the physical plane. Makes a real case for non-attachment doesn't it?

Regarding staff members, it is hoped that after years of entering the silence, helping others learn to communicate with Creator and performing last rituals on the dying, these individuals will have attained a very developed vibratory rate of their own. (Acts of service to others being very positive,) However; staff who use their position and influence to exploit the unaware will no doubt influence their vibratory rate in a negative way.

One might think that staff members work themselves out of a job as new creator becomes "aware". But no worries, there are always new creators appearing and other responsibilities to tend to.

LAW

Some people think they would like to live without laws, without regard for others, just do what they choose, whenever they choose. It would be survival of the fittest.

Both religion and law of the land have developed guidelines and parameters for behavior within society. If we live within these parameters, and play well with others, we can live without sanctions. When we get outside those parameters and impact other people in a negative way, there are sanctions up to and including termination for not acting right. Creation did this so that we can develop an appreciation for "cause and effect."

As a child, if we slap another child or we don't play well with another, we may get a spanking or a time out, something we don't want or like. As we become adults, we get time outs, which would be prison, or if we kill somebody we can be terminated which means we won't ever get to play with other people, ever.

The point is that early on as creators we have to know that there are ramifications of our decisions. As we mature as creators, we learn about cause and effect early so that when we are creating the world we live in, we already have an appreciation for the impact of our decisions. This will ultimately make us better creators.

From a creation point of view, there is no such thing as good and evil, only cause and effect. For example, consider the tsunami tragedy on the coast of India. Someone with a broader vision may consider that urban renewal. Tearing out a ghetto with disease, corruption and starting over again can be interpreted as a positive thing. Some people would call a forest fire a terrible tragedy, and it is, for those that lose homes. However, out of that tragedy we have new growth, stronger species and an improved environment.

RELATIONSHIPS AND SEX

Why do we have relationships? Because we are programed to have relationships, so we will procreate. It's all about survival of the species. I'm going to combine relationships and sex because they seem to go together many times. Simply stated, sex is about natural chemicals in our bodies, about feeling good or experiencing pleasure. What we are talking about is chemicals in our body. For example, if we are touched just skin against skin, we get a release of various chemicals that go to the brain and give us a bunch of input, very pleasurable. That's why we like to be touched.

Here is an excerpt from a book entitled *Neurolovology: the Power to Mindful Love and Sex* by Dr. Ava Cadell:

Chemical Cocktails of Romance...

"Attraction works very much like a powerful cocktail. The process of getting "turned on" through the feelings of attraction and desire is powered by various chemicals and hormones that complete an intricate recipe within the body.

If your brain is the bartender and your body the glass, the various elements are the special ingredients in the cocktail of life.

While vodka can be fine on its own, you need to bring in the added elements of peach schnapps, cranberry juice and orange juice in order to sip a little "Sex on the Beach." The brain works much the same way. You may have one basic thought ("that girl is pretty"), and then suddenly with a splash of this chemical and twist of that hormone, you're giddy with desire!

Oxytocin is like the strawberry in the strawberry daiquiri. It is released by the pituitary gland and has been linked to the formation of close social bonds because it decreases stress levels and increases trust. Vasopressin is like the tonic in the gin. It is a calming chemical secreted by the hypothalamus that fuels long-term relationship bonding.

Androgens are the Tabasco in the Bloody Mary. Testosterone is the primary sex hormone from a group called "Androgens." Produced mostly by the male testicles, it can also be produced in smaller amounts by the female ovaries. While most men produce 6 to 8 mg of testosterone a day, most women produce only 0.5 mg. Low levels of testosterone have been linked to decreased sexual desire as well as causing some men to have difficulty maintaining an erection, while high levels may increase sexual lust in both sexes. In fact, women in their reproductive years have seen their testosterone levels spike in the middle of their menstrual cycle, which helps explain why many women have reported an increased sexual appetite when they are most fertile.

Estrogens are like the cranberry juice in a Cosmopolitan. These are the sex hormones produced primarily by a female's ovaries that play a large role in the female body by stimulating the growth of sex organs, breasts and pubic hair, while also regulating the menstrual cycle. The brain of both sexes also produces estrogen, though what part this plays in male sexuality hasn't yet been established. It is believed by many researchers that it plays an important role in sexual appetite.

Nitric Oxide is the olive juice in the dirty martini. This chemical is released by the genitals during arousal. It increases blood flow to the sex organs, especially the penis.

Pheromones are the lime juice on the glass rim of a margarita. These scented hormones are found primarily in the odor- producing apocrine glands of the armpits and other areas of the body that have hair follicles. Linked to sexual attraction, research has indicated that we may select our partners by using a set of subtle smell cues, since no two people have the same odor print, with the exception of identical twins. However there is much research in progress about the exact way these hormones work, so the jury is still out.

Neurotransmitters are like the various fruits in sangria. Epinephrine, norepinephrine, dopamine, serotonin, and phenyl ethylamine (PEA) are the "BrainGasm" neurotransmitters that stimulate motivation and drive. After playing a minor role in the initial phase of love, it is really in the second stage ("Adventure") that they take the spotlight and work to help the brain feel balanced. Epinephrine and norepinephrine are responsible for the feelings of an "adrenaline rush," with high levels associated with anxiety and low levels with depression."

When we share a kiss, we experience an array of chemical reactions that put our bodies on high alert! The brain lights up with a kiss, and the more intimate we get with sex, the more dope is released in our brain, which induces more pleasure.

That's why the start of a relationship is so great. Like a brand-new addict, we go from, didn't have any of this "feel good stuff" to "Wow! I'm really liking this." It doesn't take much to get a real buzz off it. We are enjoying our experience, so we decide to stay with this special "other" for a while to see where this goes.

Here is another excerpt from a book *The Brain in Love,* by Daniel G. Amen, M.D.:

"Sex is best in the context of a committed, loving relationship. Anthropologist Helen Fisher writes, "Do not copulate with people you do not want to fall in love with, because you might do just that." Sex bonds you to others, and in some cases, if you are not careful and thoughtful, it can put you in bondage to others."

After we have been in a relationship for a while, some of the buzz leaves us. We don't get that real buzz experience after a few years of being close. Things mellow out as we enter a routine. Many couples find this experience very fulfilling and stay together for years. Others don't, but either way, the end of the relationship always comes.

That's the sad part because like any other chemical addiction there's a withdrawal. We experience loss as we miss the physical and mental sensations related to the relationship. That's what makes breaking up so hard to do. Some people actually die from this; they die of a "broken heart." It's so difficult, truly gut wrenching at times, but that's how creation designed us. We always look for relationships. We want to be with others.

It's a rare individual that is alone all the time. Many people are not alone because they want to be there. They are there because something has either happened that made them not want to experience that high again because of fear of the low, such as loss of a loved one. Sometimes situations happen where people are isolated and alone. Not because they want to be there, it's just that is how it is for them, like the old or otherwise challenged. Consider that there is much learning and experiencing that occurs while a person is alone.

Next we will discuss our "ethereal body," the energy field surrounding us that mimics our physical body. (Check out auras).

The physical portion of male and female orgasm is obvious. However; what is not so obvious is what happens in the non-physical realm during this same moment. When the female experiences orgasm, there is a very pleasant "emotional release" that exits her lowest energy chakra (root chakra). When the male experiences orgasm, there is a similar release from his root chakra. His release, however, is directed into the female adding his male energy to her already large store of female energy located just below the navel, called the lower Tan Tien. The male release is very pleasurable also, but it challenges him in a different way: it takes a lot of energy from the male to produce the physical aspects of orgasm, in addition to the energy released from the energy body, both being received by the female. This is why after sex, many females experience a warm sensation in their lower abdomen accompanied by feeling energized. The male, while feeling satisfied and warm, may be experiencing depleted energy and want to rest.

I suggest to you that the non-physical energy released by the male into the female during sex creates a "bridge" from the non- physical to the physical. This is the point where the Divine Essence of the one returning to the physical plane enters the female = conception.

Every Woman Deserves...

- Every woman deserves a man who calls her "Baby";
- Kisses like he means it;
- Holds her like he never wants to let go;
- Doesn't cheat or lie;
- Wipes her tears when she cries;
- Doesn't make her jealous of other women,
- Instead makes other women jealous of her;
- Isn't scared to let his friends know how he really feels about her;
- And lets her know how much he really LOVES HER

(Author Unknown)

I would like to end this discussion of re-lationships and sex on a high note. Re-call in prior chapters we talked about us each having a unique vibratory signature and we know that our physical body is surrounded by an "energy body". It's my thought that as we go about our lives, i.e., talking, standing in line at the grocery, etc., our energy fields are in contact with each other. As our vibratory signatures contact each other, we receive impressions from the other person. Our impressions are influenced by how close to our vibratory signature the other persons' signature is.

This resonance of vibratory signature is why we are instantly attracted to some, or repelled by others, (dissimilar vibra-tory signature). The closer the vibrato-ry signature is to matching our own, the more we are attracted to that per-son. This is where we get the concept of a "soulmate". When the other per-sons' vibratory signature is very close to our own we are extremely attracted!

WORK

People need work so they can find their creative expression. People work not only to provide for themselves and loved ones but to add meaning to life by being productive. Work is important. Everyone is where they are, whether they like it or not. They find work, or whatever they happen to do eventually. Even if it looks as if they don't have any work, they do. All of us find a way to get what we need to survive. The struggle to survive is part of the nature of life on the physical plane. Creation designed it this way. Because satisfying our needs is a huge motivator to develop the tools needed to practice our skills by manifesting things in our lives. Unfortunately, until we are skilled manifesters we sometimes get things we don't want. Another tough part about life is that by our thoughts, we attract situations to learn or experience things, that we still need to work on. Until we gain control of our thoughts, use free will effectively, and learn to discipline ourselves to choose wisely, we will continue to struggle. In our Western culture, old people don't get much respect. They are pretty much cast aside. Members of the older generation throughout their lives have created, evolved, and have a lifetime of learning. Many are aware of their thoughts and are adept creators.

I am part of this senior segment of society. Our job, our work if you will, as we reach our mature years, is not so much physical but cerebral. In that, we should be surrounding those we love with love and protection, good vibrations. As a group we must try to affect world events and influence outcome of situations in the world by using our creative abilities.

We are powerful, thought energy generators. With knowledge comes responsibility. As responsible creators, it is up to us to help clean up the planet and influence nations to cooperate and work together for the common good. The opportunity to work to make the world a better place for our children may be the highest and best work of our lives.

I will take one moment to state my credo:

If not me, who? If not now, when?

This is a call to all conscious creators to spend time daily, asking desperately for positive outcomes globally and locally. Only as we use our creative ability effectively and wisely can we hope to have happy lives and evolve as children of creation.

INTEGRITY

It's been said that integrity is what you do when nobody's looking. I think it is so important. Everyone learns this on their own. I know from personal experience. I recall so many shortcomings, so many failures and things I wish I had done differently. Again by creator's design, part of the evolving process is an acceptance of these failures and being able to love myself as I am. Integrity includes not only how I act, but how I treat other people, how I operate within the world.

Integrity has a lot to do with karma, when we do the right thing or do things well. The creative thought energy that we generate, goes out into creation to manifest, but in addition the vibratory energy that we used during the process becomes part of our own unique vibratory signature. If we put out crap, we're going to get a whole load of crap coming back. If you put out good, you'll get all kinds of good coming back. I know from my own personal experiences that is how things work; one leaves a bitter taste in your mouth, the other sweet.

HEAVEN AND HELL

Throughout life our subconscious keeps track of every thought we have throughout our entire existence on this physical plane. When we die, we leave our physical body and our Divine Essence heads out into creation. Creation is made up of levels, like onion skins or the thousand petal Lotus the ancients talk about. As an example, I relate each petal   to a radio frequency. In creation there is an infinite number of radio frequencies, and each one of these frequencies is a level of existence, with an infinite number of levels of awareness within it.

It's been said we create our own heaven or hell. When we die our Divine Essence, which is non-physical, leaves the physical plane and heads out into creation at the speed of thought. At this moment the impact of the Law of Attraction becomes apparent.

Our lifetime, as recorded by subconscious, results in a specific vibratory rate unique to each of us. When we head out into creation, in accordance to the Law of Attraction, our Divine Essence will instantly go to the layer of creation that it resonates with. If the layer of creation that resonates with us is not such a great place, welcome to Hell. This is the layer of creation that resonates with the unique vibratory rate we earned over a lifetime of thought, choices and action. This is where we will be until we are given the opportunity to spend time on the physical plane again to learn and experience, thereby changing our vibratory rate.

If our unique vibratory rate is of a more positive or higher rate, then we go to a level of existence in creation which resonates with this vibration.

How long do we have to continue this heaven and hell existence? This cycle of working on the physical plane

and returning to the non- physical continues until we reach a point where
our positive and negative are in bal-
ance. By then our unique vibratory rate
again resonates with that of Creator.
Then we stay right there with Creator.

How long does the process take to
again resonate with Creator? It takes as
long as it takes, possibly thousands of
lifetimes, thousands of returns to the
physical level. One must remember that
we exist in the infinite, plenty of time.

One might ask "Do I believe there's
more than one physical level within the
infinite levels of existence?" I think it
would be a real stretch to say that there
are not many other physical levels where
we can learn and experience. Not all of
them look like the one we are experiencing here on this earth, but there are many
different types and many different levels.

We are children of creator. As we mature and evolve as creators and become more adept at creating, we are given challenges to help us grow as creators. When we are fully developed creators, we will eventually have our own "creation." We as individuals will be the creator of this new creation, with all the duties and responsibilities inherent to the task.

Our goal is to emulate our creator and become Creator with a capital C in our own right. Then we will be in the position of creating our own children and so on. Thus the cycle continues infinitely: Everyone is born, grows, and eventually becomes Creator. This is our design, our nature, and our goal. So must it be.

One last thought for this section. Consider that in the non-physical there are no secrets, nothing is hidden. All are connected via the love vibration. Everyone is aware of everything others have ever thought or experienced. Something to think about.

Thoughts on Creation

DEATH AND DYING

Lots of people talk about the circle of life and how death is just a natural aspect of life. Maybe they have never considered or really don't understand what they are talking about. Given that creation contains everything and there can be nothing outside of creation, we never actually die. When we experience physical death and our Divine Essence leaves this level of physical existence, the physical parts of our body decompose and are recycled again. We see so often in nature everything being circular and being recycled. The same is true for our body it goes back to its most basic components; molecules and becomes other things.

Like other things in our world, we go through a change of state. So we are still here: just like steam turns into water, people turn into their most basic components and are recycled. When the immortal part of us, our Divine Essence, is released from the physical body, we are able to embrace our true vibratory nature and return to the great ocean of creation. Consider the ocean, as vast as it is, is made up of individual drops of water. We are each individual drops of water. We carry with us our complete history of learning and experience when we return in the non-physical to take our place in creation.

At death, after the Divine Essence has departed, the energy body which surrounds us is redistributed back to the physical plane where its vibration is added to the global vibratory rate. (This is because the slower physical plane vibration can't exit the physical plane.)

Some religions think it is very important that a persons' final thoughts be of a positive nature. Because these final thoughts as they are leaving the physical plane and exiting out into creation are very influential about where they end up. One of the strongest emotions we can possibly have is the death emotion. Therefore; it could have a significant influence on our unique vibratory rate. And as you recall our unique vibratory rate defines where we end up in the non-physical.

That is why it is so important for family and friends to be supportive, loving, and caring. We must give people making their exit an opportunity to focus, to think happy thoughts, loving thoughts as they exit the physical level of existence.

Some organizations perform a "last ritual" with the soon to die. This is designed to help the departing one to be calm, focus their mental state and hopefully exit to a better place in the   non-physical. During the ritual the person performing the ritual will add their emotional plea for the person dying. This may be of great help to the exiting person.

One day all people will become evolved creators. It has been said that an evolved creator can influence tens and hundreds of thousands of other people. This is done through their actions, by observing their power, and by others experiencing their vibratory rate. The vibratory rate of an evolved creator actually raises the vibratory rate of all who come in contact with them.

Someday, it will be common for evolved creators to willfully choose the end of their time. They will voluntarily give up their physical existence. The difference between this noble act and normal death is: "Normal death" is when we run out to the end of our time, the person closes their eyes, quits breathing and eventually the heart stops. The Divine Essence departs the physical body on the final breath, to return to the non-physical, and the physical body starts to decompose. Normal death is a passive act.

What I'm suggesting for the evolved creator is as follows: Exiting the physical plane in this manner would be a very active act. The evolved soul will decide it is time for them to exit the physical plane of existence, for the common good. They give up their life on the physical plane, to release all the high vibrations contained within their physical bodies to raise the vibratory rate on this plane of existence. All the good parts of them stay on the physical level to be redistributed back to the global vibration.

For example, Jesus Christ, through his death, affected all of this physical plane and made the world a better place. That's the impact that I'm talking about.

So once again, leaving this physical plane of existence will be a noble act, a final gift, of all the good and all that is positive in a person. They will take their lifetime of accumulated high vibrations and through their own will, discipline and love, lay it down for the common good. I don't think there is a nobler act or a life better spent than that.

A discussion of death and dying often begs the question: What about those who remain on the physical plane after death? This is in reference to ghosts and other non-physical entities who stay on this physical level of existence. It's my thought that these beings either don't realize that they have died, or they have some attachment to this plane which keeps their vibratory rate the same as this plane of existence.

These beings must stay at this level until they realize that they have died or escape the attachment that is holding them here. Once they accept or understand, the subconscious is able to determine their true vibratory rate, and they will move to the level of infinity resonate with their unique vibratory signature.

MAN AS CREATOR

I submit to you that it is mans' ability to create that separates us from the rest of the animals in creation. It is also what gives us the ability to change our environment and the responsibility to do so with awareness. To create is to generate thought even in an abstract sense. When we think, it generates an electrical signal through our brain which can be measured.

What cannot be measured by us yet is the non-physical energy created by our mind when we create, which is all the time. Consider that when we create, we send messages to Creator via the subconscious and the Love Vibration. And depending on the clarity and the power of our thoughts, our thought creations manifest on the physical plane.

It is through our hard work and commitment, including time spent in the silence, serious personal work on our own biases and limiting thoughts that we eventually become adept creators.

With knowledge comes responsibility, and we have many learning experiences as we evolve as creators. This impacts our world and our lives as well as the lives of those around us. This is an interesting thought. As each of us evolve and become creators, at some point in the infinite (after we have had infinite learning experiences and infinite practice creating and manifesting) we each become creators of universes and cosmos. This is not to be confused with the ultimate creation or Creator, but as children of creation we will become creators. Yes, we become creators of universes and cosmos and never-ending, expanding creation---something to think about.

WARRIOR

We are all warriors in my opinion. The journey from being clueless to the master creator is very tough. Like warriors we must be resilient, resourceful and tenacious. When we get knocked down or disappointed, we must get back up. Through the evolutionary process of becoming a fully developed creator, we get beat up and sometimes have a very difficult time learning some lessons.

I think this is natural, and something that everyone will go through, everyone will experience everything. The handicapped this time around will get to experience the gifts of those that are the tremendously successful. Another time we will experience extreme poverty and sickness even terrible suffering.

That's why it takes great courage, discipline and will to do the work on this plane of existence. But this is the work we came here to do, what we were born to do, to experience and learn, to perfect our skills at creating. It occurs to me that another skill we are here to learn is to love. How to love ourselves and others, to give back when appropriate and to become a positive vibratory force. Thereby; becoming a creator in that aspect of our self as well.

SELF-IMAGE AND SELF TALK

In our manifesting practice, we have to be constantly aware of sabotaging our efforts. This is where self-image and self-talk come in. We need to love ourselves and accept ourselves as we are—imperfect. The first time I tried to dance, l was not a very good dancer, but as I become a better dancer and I made fewer mistakes, my concept of myself as a dancer improved, my self-talk improved and the overall experience got better. Now I enjoy dancing and can teach others.

Early in the learning about manifesting, people need to be aware of their self-talk and even change their self-talk to become more supportive and positive. It's easy to talk negatively to ourselves and call ourselves stupid or inept. We must eliminate all these negative thoughts and words. We must discipline ourselves to be more accepting and loving.

Consider changing your self-talk to something like this:

"I am a child of Creator; I am a creator. I will become good at this. I can do this. My Creator wants me to do this, and I will learn how to do this. This is my work. This is what I do. This is what I am."

It may be slow going in some cases, yet other parts of it will be relatively easy to learn. We must see ourselves as capable and as deserving. In our minds' eye see ourselves becoming creators of our destiny as children of creation. It is our birthright and destiny.

MANIFESTING

Our ultimate goal is to become manifesters or creators. Similar to when children and adolescents turn into adults and then into sages and masters. We have changed through our many trips to the physical plane. We likely started out as basic elements. We then worked our way from random elements into some more complex material, which would be rocks and minerals. Then we worked our way through the plant and animal kingdoms, this time in the physical, we inhabit a human body with the ability for abstract thought. Now we are ready to take the intensive course on creating.

With a physical body and brain we actually get two gifts, the ability to think in abstract and free will. These two gifts enable us to develop our creative power and choose our own destiny. With the ability to manifest whatever we want, we eventually   become creators of our own universes and cosmos. On the physical plane, we develop and use tools in our manifesting. Imagination is one of those tools. We all use imagination all the time, we don't think of it as part of creating, but it's an integral part. Without imagination we would not be creators. We use imagination from childhood throughout our lives as a creative tool. I suppose it could be said that thinking in the abstract and using our imagination, in this context, are the same.

As adults we learn the technique of meditation. This is a tool to develop the mental muscle to concentrate, develop the will and discipline that it takes to manifest things.

Visualization is one of our tools we use. Imagination and visualization are similar but distinctly different. Imagination is used to come up with an idea. Visualization is used to get a well-defined image, concept or feeling of whatever it is we want to manifest.

These are the tools that we are here to develop. We practice creating our own lives whether we like it or not, all the time. We affect others around us, and that is our task. We will take the various skills learned and apply them to manifesting things. If we are not successful in our manifesting, if we don't get it, if we get lazy, if we do not make good decisions, we get to keep trying until we learn the skill. We must learn to rely on our own ability to carry on and live our lives as fully functioning creators.

Consider this about drugs to enhance creativity. I don't think drugs are a useful tool for developing our manifesting abilities. Drugs are artificial and not reliable, many deliver us to places we don't want to be. And we all have the ability to do this on our own.

When manifesting consider that the subconscious will attempt to attract whatever we tell it to. Remember, subconscious does not judge or edit our thoughts it just takes them as presented. However; know that your manifesting will be much more productive if subconscious has a clear well defined thought to work with. It is up to the conscious mind to fully consider what we want and to choose wisely.

This is the free will part again. When choosing wisely I encourage you to take your time to discover what is actually desired. For example, asking for money, do I really want to be wealthy, with all the burdens and responsibilities that come with wealth? Or do I just want to be happy, feel loved and accepted? Do I really want this one special object of my affections? Or do I just want to "feel" all the good feelings I imagine will come with the relationship, or not?

Regardless what you decide to ask for consider this. Creator wants us to be happy. Creator has limitless resources to give us whatever we want. But it is on us to communicate effectively.

Consider the following two scenarios:

First scenario, a child approaches their mother, who loves them dearly. The child with head down, looking away, in a small indistinct mumble says something. Mom can't understand what the child wants. So likely not a happy ending.

Scenario two, the child approaches the mother, smiling, says "I love you Mama". Then while looking in her eyes with full expectation of getting what is requested says, "Mama, may I have a cookie?" Hmm, which child do you think got the cookie? In fact, likely the child who asked clearly and distinctly with love, probably got two cookies.

This brings up another thought. I encourage you to end your manifesting session with the following phrase or something like it. "These are my requests, please grant them or something even better, for the highest and best good of all concerned". This allows creation with its much larger vision of what is good for us to work without limits to make us happy. When we set limits for creation to work within, we are sabotaging our manifesting efforts from the beginning. Think about it, very important!

We must become the author of our experience, creator of our existence. Again, we will all get to this point eventually because we will continue returning to the physical plane until we do. Remember, man made up the concept of time, creation has no end. So relax, take your time, no worries.

HEALING

Healing provides us an opportunity, as new creators, to practice many different things that we need to learn. One would be to practice loving each other. There has to be an element of compassion, love and care for another to send healing energy. Whether it's actually laying on of hands or remote healing using visualization and emotion to send energy to someone. Any type of healing work tests us and helps us develop our ability to focus, use our will-power, and emotion in our manifesting for it to be effective. The mechanics of going through a healing session offer many opportunities to become better creators.

Following are a few of my experiences with healing and manifesting. These are included to show the scope and power of a well-defined thought, wisely chosen, sent out into creation with strong emotion.

A great man once said, "When you do what I have done, you will be able to do what I do". (Yes, he's talking to you).

My first experience in conscious healing was with my brother's cat, GC. GC had been diagnosed with feline leukemia, usually a death sentence. At first opportunity I took the cat in my arms, focused on breathing healing energy into my heart space, and then sent it to GC seeing it surrounding him in healing light. After a time, I stopped the visualization and moved on, leaving creation to do the work. GC did die, however; it was ten years later after a long happy life.

Another time a friend of mine was distraught due to loss of her job. She was working to manifest another job for herself. She asked for my assistance which of course I said I would do what I could. During my next meditation session, I once again filled my heart space with healing, loving, white light and saw her surrounded with it. Then I asked Creator to help her to find another job, good as or better than, the one she had before. Then I let it go so that creation could do its' work. Within a few days a job even better for her, with higher pay, came from a totally un-expected source. Another happy ending.

The following is an example using the same technique of filling my heart space with love and white light, then visualizing surrounding the person with love and heal-ing light, while making request to Creator.

Note: In all cases requests to Cre-ator were made with strong emotion.

It's my experience that tears accompany a heartfelt plea. In one case a man had pancreatic cancer, once again a death sentence. He had already done two rounds of chemo, out of desperation he agreed to one more round. It was about this time a friend described his situation and asked for assistance. Same technique, asked for the highest and best good for all concerned and Creator's will be done. A couple of weeks later the friend call to report a "miracle". During routine testing to see how the chemo was progressing there was no cancer detected. Chemo was stopped and more testing was done. An amazed doctor told the man that as reluctant as he was to use the term, cured, there was no sign of cancer! He was cured! The man within weeks found a job and resumed normal life after a three year hiatus.

Another case, involved a woman who was also filled with cancer, as requested I offered up my request to Creator using the same technique and again ending with "for the highest and best good for all concerned". This case felt different, so I asked that if it was her time that she be taken with compassion and love. Then let the visualization go so creation could go to work unhindered. The woman's condition continued to decline. In less than a month she passed, surrounded by family at home. She was smiling.

Know this about healing...we make requests and help out in many ways, but.....

Creation Does the Healing!

PERSONAL

RESPONSIBILITY

As we come up through various levels of existence from mineral to plant, animal to person, we are cared for by our Creator. When we become people obviously Creator still supplies all of our needs. Have no doubt, that it is our Creator that supplies all of our needs all the time. However, there is an element of personal responsibility that comes with being human on this physical plane of existence.

We are given the task and the responsibility to make good choices for ourselves, to take care of our bodies, and to take care of our families and our world. With knowledge comes responsibility. As we become more effective creators we learn how to influence. How to manifest what we want whether it's wealth, knowledge or more relationships. We are always tempted to become greedy, to want all the money, to want all the power. We have to guard against this constantly so that we don't become seduced and become part of the problem rather than part of the solution.

As we age and our physical bodies decline, as long as we have our minds, we can be powerful thought generators. Our thoughts can influence our world in a positive manner. Elders are some of the most powerful people as they enter the silence with their greater willpower, and great skill at creating.

Being creator...that is our challenge as we age...to become the best creators that we can for the common good. That would be our final noble act for the common good, to responsibly spend our time and energy to make the world a better place.

FAMILY ROLES

Once again we are here to learn as we experience birth and infancy, adolescence, childhood, adulthood, and old age. There are so many opportunities to learn and experience, both positive and negative. That is why we have family units and our place within those units. On the larger scale, we have our place in the community, the nation and the world. All these different positions require different activities of us to fulfill our roles; they require us to think, learn, experience, manifest, and influence and to be responsible for ourselves and others. That is why we have these learning opportunities. It is all about learning and experience, and we keep all of these in our memory of our infinite existence.

As we grow in our roles our influence and responsibility for ourselves and others grows, also. Progress toward being a fully   evolved person is why we have these learning opportunities. It is all about learning and experience. As we live our lives a record of everything is kept in our subconscious in the form of vibrations. When we exit the physical plane the total of all our vibrations is tallied and a unique vibratory signature is found. This unique vibration is what finds our place in creation as we pass into the non-physical. See chapter on Heaven and Hell.

CHARITY AND GIVING

When we experience compassion for someone, when we see them suffering, we want to relieve that suffering. That is a learning experience for us as future creators, to feel compassion and to want to help. Regarding charity and giving, I submit to you that a complete circuit is required. In order for there to be giving, someone has to receive. Both sides of the equation are equally important.

So, once again, in order for us to give, there has to be someone to receive. If we're analytical about it, we could say that the receiving person is just in the receiving position. They shouldn't be looked down upon, that's just where they are at this point in time, but without them we could not give.

Without receivers we could not experience compassion and feel motivated to help them. As givers there are many lessons to be learned in the process of providing healing and support to those in need. To those in need, there are an equal amount of lessons to be learned while on the receiving end of the equation. That is why we have the charitable works and poor people. It's all about learning and experience. And if we don't get it the first time around, we have to continue to experience and learn until we understand. We keep taking the class until we get it.

Now I will discuss giving and charity from a different perspective. Giving something to somebody really doesn't fix anything, it just buys time and maybe gives them hope. When you give somebody something, it proves to the receiver, that the giver thinks they can't help themselves. This robs the receiver of their self- respect if we don't appreciate the fact that they have the ability to help themselves. It puts them in a subordinate position of being defective, incapable and limited. No one could possibly enjoy life feeling this way.

The wise giver, in my opinion, tries to do more than buy time. The wise giver looks for ways to empower the receiver. Education is one thing that comes to mind. There are many kinds of education all leading to the same goal of helping the needy to help themselves if possible. To empower receivers to make their own way, while building their self-esteem, respect and confidence to become creators of their own lives, is wise giving.

This begs the question "what about receivers who are in such a situation that there is no getting better or hope for improvement?" I suggest that we feel compassion and support these people. And do it with understanding that sometime it will be us in the receiver position. Remember everyone gets to experience everything. Therefore; I suggest that we treat receivers with respect and dignity acknowledging that they are experiencing a difficult time.

If we give for the wrong reason, however well meaning, it may be an attempt to control the other person. For example; when a parent gives excessively to a child their whole life, the child may be handicapped socially or financially, because they don't have the skills that the parent has. The parent is making the child dependent.

Many times the parent is hoping to control the child. They have done so many things for them, they hope the child will love them. And yet the child is saying "thanks for nothing" because they have no skills. They will always be dependent on someone to provide for them. This puts the child in a very vulnerable position.

What a disservice as parents! We want to teach them the skills required to do well in the world. The skills I am referring to are the tools of the creator. Teaching a child how to meditate early is a good start. Showing a child by example, the benefits of daily meditation is good, I suggest sit together and meditate. Other skills of visualization and opportunities to be creative are things that we can do for our children that don't cost a thing, yet pay huge rewards in life.

KARMA

Karma, what do you think? Does creation hold us accountable for our creations? Free will for creators is a double edged sword. We are given the keys to the kingdom, but when we make poor choices, then often bad things happen to us.

As we become more adept at creating and make better choices, our karmic debt seems to lessen and we do better. It's all on us! We enjoy being creators, but sometimes we don't enjoy reaping the rewards of what we sow.

Some say that creation punishes us; I say no it does not. All creation does is let us enjoy the fruits of our labor. If we don't know better than to manifest things that are not good for us, many times there are painful sanctions for us to experience, so we learn.

We need to use our tools of will and discipline to keep us aware of our thoughts and to think thoughts about what we do want to attract into our lives, what we do want to manifest in our lives. I suggest, that the biggest motivator for us to become better creators is to avoid the pain of making bad choices. Perhaps that's the point of a negative experience. We learn so much more from a negative experience than we do a happy experience.

So that's why I don't think creation punishes. All creation did was give us free will and the ability to create whatever we want. What we do with our gifts is our responsibility.

Glossary of Terms

Creator --- The original creative force which provides for us, sustains us and loves us as its children

Creation -- All the infinite levels of existence

Divine Essence -- Our immortal self

Physical Plane of Existence -- Existence unaware of the love vibration due to our different vibratory rate.

Non-Physical Plane of Existence -- Existence aware of the love vibration due to our similar vibratory rate

Awareness -- The ability to sense and recognize other vibrations

Level of Awareness -- Awareness within our Level of Existence

Level(s) of Awareness --Infinite levels within a Level of Existence

Monkey Mind -- Refers to the out-of-control undisciplined mind

Free Will -- The ability to choose between options

Will -- Same as will power, we use this in creating to stay focused, continue with a task to completion. Used in concert with self- disciplined

My Meditation Technique

Find a spot where I won't be disturbed for as long as I intend to be in the silence.

Take a meditative posture, I set on floor Indian style, but can be any comfortable position. I close my eyes.

Think about why I am entering the silence, asking for information or guidance, giving thanks, relaxing, other.

Say My Invocation.

Focus on breath for a moment to calm myself.

Three to six Om's to raise my vibratory rate.

Assume attitude of active listening. As thoughts pop up, and they do, bring mind back to silent.

Stay as long as want, give thanks and leave the silence.

My Healing Technique

- Find a place I won't be distracted or interrupted
- Assume a comfortable position
- Calm my mind, maybe Om or breathing exercise
- Say My Invocation
- Observe the breath, on in breath I see healing energy entering my heart chakra, each breath brings more and more until I feel ready to send it out
- I switch my visualization to object of healing. I may look at a specific point or see all of object or think of their name
- With heart felt emotion (very important) I send the healing energy to the object, surrounding in white light and healing energy. No worries… the energy knows where to go if I don't. As I send the healing white light I ask Creator with emotion, fervently, emotionally (usually comes with

tears) for healing or whatever for object. Hold this visualization asking clearly and distinctly for what is desired until "feels" completed.

- End the visualization and sending of energy.
- Thank Creator and, very important, end session with "I ask for these things or something even better, for the good of all concerned.

My Invocation

My Father, who is creation, sacred is
your name.

Your kingdom surrounds and fills
me, your will is upon the earth as it is
throughout the universe.

You provide for all my needs, you forgive
me of my offenses, as I forgive those who
offend me.

You do not allow me to enter into mate-
rialism, but separate me from error.

Yours is the kingdom and the power and
the song from age to age.

Sealed in Faithfulness

CPSIA information can be obtained
at www.ICGtesting.com
Printed in the USA
FFHW010825210519
52580918-58048FF